Prepper's Guide:

List Of Items You Can Barter after the Collapse With Useful Tips

Table of Contents

Introduction

Welcome to Prepper's Stockpile Guide: Items You Can Barter After the Collapse When Cash Is Worthless, a book designed to help you gather the most profitable and sustainable items in the event that cash loses its value. For over a few decades, many have speculated that the dollar will eventually collapse in their time. In the past few years, this number of individuals has gone up due to the poor choices the authorities of the world has changed. This is why knowing what materials you can barter will be vital if the dollar truly does collapse. Let's begin.

Chapter 1 – What Not To Keep

Let's talk about what will be useless when SHTF even though they have a lot of bartering value right now. I prefer to start off with what you don't need and build from there so that any person that wants to start a situation knows the standard starting point for the best possible outcome. For some, this may be incredibly unpleasant to hear.

Tender Bills

The most useless of them all, paper money. The bill is representative of money or rather the gold that the current government you are in has during the time that you are living. Since the gold is a precious resource, it has a finite value in the world. The problem with a finite value is that it is very difficult to go beyond what you have so the world invented paper money, which is why so many people are in debt. Once SHTF, the paper money is useless because there isn't any gold to back it up, but even then pure gold can't save you in some situations.

Precious Metals

Most survivalists will tell you that precious metals, like gold, have no place in the environment after SHTF. The only problem is that they are situationally wrong about this. It's not their fault really, it actually takes a great mind with a lot of foresight to see where such metals could take place in such an environment. When they talk about "SHTF" they tend to assume there will be no power, which is simply not true. If the entire grid were to shut off right now, there would still be people with power and these people own Solar Panels. Solar Panels will become absolutely precious unless someone figures out a way to make them without a lab involved.

What do the precious metals have to do with solar panels? Solar panels depreciate over time, but it takes precious metals to fix the parts they run off of. Therefore, things like copper (a not so precious, precious metal) conduct the electricity that allows the solar panel to produce power. However, even if we weren't talking about solar panels, we would still have water power and wind power. They may not produce as much energy, but they do still produce energy.

But what about gold? Will it still have value? Yes and no, depending on your situation. See, if everything becomes a you versus the world environment then yes as gold won't feed you, clothe you, or bathe you. However, if you still have some modicum of government in your area, whether it be leftovers or civilian formed, they will often still value gold as a trading currency. The odds of this actually being the case is so small that it could compete with the lottery in a game of chance. It's not something you will likely want to keep.

Large Guns

You do not need things like rifles, and anyone who tells you this hasn't had to survive in any location for a long period of time. Pistols are cheaper in literally every way when compared to any type of gun. Shotguns are only useful if you know how to make your own shotgun bullets without electric-powered machinery and have the materials. The problem with both of these is that many people will kill you to obtain ammunition, which is why, in a survival situation, having a stockpile of it is a very bad idea.

No, what you really want to invest in when SHTF is blades, bows, and mallets. The problem with guns is the fact that they run out, but a well-groomed katana or short sword will take years to break. Even more so, being able to make these weapons will have people coming to your door on a regular basis without you needing to do much more than make some shabby blades. In these times, you will be living in the medieval age and those that can make weapons are not only left alone, usually protected, but also given a lot of product for just a weapon. It's even better if you can make more than just swords, like bows and hammers. These will be essential tools that the average person will need in order to survive during times like these and the person who can make them will be afforded the greatest of bartering material.

Likewise, this will naturally help you survive in the long run. Meanwhile, large guns will run out as bullets for such guns will run out very quickly. Until then, you should keep a pistol on hand to take care of such cases because it does take time for all the bullets to disappear. If you really want a gun for the long hall, then you should learn how to make your own bullets for your pistol and ensure you have the proper material to make it.

Chapter 2 – Knowledge

Knowledge will be the most valuable bartering resource you have because most people didn't pick up a survival book. Needless to say, libraries will be the most important sources of knowledge, but MANY people will avoid them. You see, people are a lot like sheep in the fact that if they don't see others going to it for survival, they're less likely to do so. If the average peasant didn't attend the library, what makes you think new age people will be any different? This is perhaps one thing that most movies and television series get accurate. If you can and preferably before the disaster, you need to pick up a few books:

- Herbology 101

- Electricity 101

- D.I.Y. Water Power

- D.I.Y. Wind Power

- Smithing 101

- Chemistry 101

- Common Diseases 101

- Farming 101

- First Aid 101

There are few reasons why these would be the most important. Since there is a collapse of the dollar, people will quickly find that there is a lack of medicine, power, and, given enough time, nearly anything else. Herbology, Common

Diseases, and Chemistry are subjects you want to know when making your own concoctions of medicine. Electricity will be scarce and it is one thing people will really want if they are trying to conserve food. Therefore, knowing not only electricity but also how to utilize wind and water to generate power will make you invaluable. Smithing will be how you learn to make swords, blades, and similar items that will be needed in the future. A lot of people don't know how to farm. Why would they, considering most just go to the market for their food?

These books may not be exactly titled like this, but the important thing is that you get the gist. All of these subjects will be vitally important to any group of people that are willing to band together to make their own town. However, that isn't even the depth of these books in terms of value because one thing people take for granted is ink. Once the dollar loses value, knowledge of how to return everything back to the way it was and even better will be the next best thing. When the ink stops, knowledge becomes even more of a limited resource. The worst part of this is that people who need to protect themselves from the cold will likely use books as their burning material if it is easier to get than the wood outside.

Teaching as a Commodity

Once you learn these subjects and know them well, if you can collect a community that need you then you have a rare opportunity. While you may get some devoutly religious people who might be against teaching, the odds of this happening is astronomically low. Just as you can find educational sources online, many people will trade in order to learn or have their children learn a craft. This is not only done for the sanity of the parents, but also because the more people know about something the more they can grow as a group, which is what we call collective learning.

People who want power in their house don't want to trade for someone to come fix it all the time. Instead, many will see that is more profitable to learn how to do it themselves so that they don't have to spend as much. People are usually selfish though and want to retain that knowledge for themselves, therefore they will likely not take a teaching position if there is already someone doing the teaching. Teachers in previous societies, before the invention of power, led luxurious lives because their knowledge was what paid for everything.

In Case of Emergency

If you were the one to come down with a fever of some preventable disease, you would not want to be the one who was treating yourself. This is why having someone else knowing the same material as yourself is useful. In case of an emergency, where you are the target of the emergency, you want to have taught someone else so that they can take care of it. You do not want to be in a situation where you are the only one who knows something.

Getting Back to Civilized Culture

When the dollar collapses, it will only be the people who have knowledge that can bring the world back from medieval times. You will be one of the most valuable people even if you only know the basics of the materials at hand. Think about this; it took us over two millennia to realize why washing your hands was important and a good portion of people on this planet still don't know the importance of this chore. We only discovered electricity in the past couple of centuries and only solar/wind power in the past century. These are recently discovered technologies and you will be the one who has the knowledge to prevent the rest of civilization from having to redo all of the work that we did for over a couple centuries. If you know this technology and these advancements, within a decade you could be living in one of the only cities on the planet that still has things like air conditioning, refrigeration, and a lot of other things we utilize in our daily lives.

While there are temporary bartering items, as we will talk about in the next couple of chapters, being knowledgeable in vital areas of studies will be the best bartering item that you have in the long run. Not only will you be the only one to still have power, but, if you get a community around you, you will be the only person who doesn't really need to do much in order to survive because the people around you support you due to the knowledge you have and the vital items you can provide.

Chapter 3 – Fuel

The first thing you tend to see in almost every survival movie, like Mad Max, is that the world goes crazy over gas. In a short bit of time, this will be true as people mainly rely on gas to do a lot of the things they like. We'll talk about that and some other, more reasonable, options.

Gas and Coal

As I've said, many movies depict a short time when people are absolutely nuts over gasoline, but this will, in reality, only be for a short amount of time. The reason why it will be short is because gas is not renewable and once cash stops, so too does anything that cash buys, like gas flowing into this country. The truth of the matter is that there is only enough gas in this country to last us for maybe a year or two. Therefore, if everyone is looking for gas then it will be a short sale and you should definitely sell.

This includes anything that has secondary gas components, like propane, coal, and hydrogen. These chemicals will be the secondary target of the market because it is flammable. This market will be relatively small though as many people don't know how to retrofit a car to utilize such forms of energy.

Why People will Want Fuel

Once cash stops, so too does anything vital that we use for outside information, like the internet and television. Since there is no pay, many people will find themselves in the struggle to survive rather than trying to run a news network.

This means that people will search for areas that do have power in hopes that they don't have to survive from day to day. This is a natural instinct for people who are not used to surviving. Even when fuel runs out, people will still try to find the "miracle" city that still has power.

Solar Power

Solar fuel, or rather solar power, will be the third type of energy resource people will go after. A lot of people realize that, while that can't get as much energy from it as they would via gas, it is still a viable source when it comes to powering things like refrigeration. This is not a material you will likely want to store a lot of as it tends to take up quite a bit of room.

Instead, what you wanna try and build (only if you are in a *nice* community) is a solar farm. This would be where you buy a solar panel as often as you can in order to build for more than just one house. If you have a solar farm then you can charge for the power and ensuring that you know how to maintenance it will also ensure that you keep getting that power.

The only problem with this type of fuel is that you won't be able to have it during the day. However, we will talk about why such fuel sources are only a temporary solution.

Wind Power

Wind is the weakest, but the most readily available energy source. Essentially all you need is a turbine attached to the middle of a fan, point it towards the wind, and you have a power source. However, unless you have a lot of these then you will find that you won't have much more than enough to power small devices.

Water Power

Water is king of both of these, provided you have a free flowing river that you can put a lot of them in. It is the same concept as the wind, but you're using water instead. Since water flows faster than the wind and since the flow of water is not the same as wind, you can usually build a water wheel farm very quickly.

The steam engine is another option, but you need to have something like fire to constantly boil water and then someone collecting water all the time. Essentially, the problem with a steam engine is that you would have to have someone constantly keeping an eye on the water level and the wood level. You would not be able to grow wood at the same amount of time that it takes to burn it, so you could build one but unless you live in the woods, you would have a couple weeks of power at most.

Why People will Want Power

Most people will want power for primarily selfish reasons like taking a shower, cooking without wood, or being able to listen to music. Power generally makes average tasks a lot easier, but it is also not something that is necessary to survive. After all, many survivalists go days to weeks without a single bit of wattage in their lives. The human mind is a survival machine, however, which means that it will take advantage of anything that makes its life easier. This is why the majority of people will want power.

Why Fuel is only a Temporary Solution unless you Expand

Turbine Generators are the real problem here and building them when you have no power is dang near impossible. Sure, you can build a windmill to churn grain, but to produce usable electricity you need a turbine generator. Turbine Generators are made of metals like copper and steel, which means you will want to stock up on a lot of them if you want to use fuel as a bartering point or if you just want to continue having power. The problem comes with trying to build more of them when there is no gas-powered stations keeping the electricity going anymore.

You see, turbines are not difficult to build because all a *turbine* is is just a fan that turns some metal. This makes it very easy to build one for water and wind. The problem is that you need to convert the spinning energy into power, which is why you need to have a turbine generator. If you want to learn how to make a turbine generator, then you need to know how to make a DC Motor or Direct Current Motor. It's confusing, right? Here's why the same device has two different names. Since the DC Motor is attached to the turbine, it is called a turbine generator.

Unless you begin using your power to build more power, then it will only be a temporary solution as the power cannot sustain itself. This includes solar power, as the power will eventually be lost given enough time.

Chapter 4 – Seeds

Perhaps the most important food item that you will want to barter off are seeds or food. The reason why it could be one over the other is really dependent on the person, but the seeds tend to go for a much higher price. This is because a seed will allow them to grow more than one crop of the food. Therefore, while it may be worth more to sell the seeds, it is *worthwhile* to just sell the food. Not only can you produce more by keeping your own seeds, but you can sell the overall product for much more than you can the individual seeds. However, there are a few stipulations.

The Type of Seed is Important

The problem with growing a crop is the fact that it is difficult to determine which foods will grow where. Even more so, it is difficult to keep food growing if you have to uproot and move to another location. Below, we'll talk about a few "Grow Anywhere" seeds as in these are seeds that will grow in nearly every livable climate that you plant them and a few others. This is not all there is, which is why you should grab a few herbology and farming books, but I've selected a couple that will take a short time to grow and a few that repeatedly give out food.

- Potatoes – 3 Months - These veggies take just three months to grow and will grow nearly everywhere. They're great for potassium, essential metals, and a few other vitamins.

- Apples – 3-4 Years - The only problem with apples is that they take a few years to grow, but once they start growing it is difficult to contain the growth. Not only will the same tree reproduce fruit repeatedly after picked, but each apple contains multiple seeds that can grow other trees. Apples can usually be grown in any livable environment.

- Pineapples – 2+ years depending on the environment - Pineapples are unique because they can grow anywhere, but they're considered a tropical fruit. The reason for this is because it is a food that grows better in hotter areas but (like the apple tree) once grown, it just keeps on giving.

- Sunflower Shoots – 12 Days - These don't take long to grow, but they cannot grow in colder environments.

- *Salad-type Vegetables* - 30 Days - Pretty much anything you might find in the salad aisle that is used as a base for the salad, like Watercress, Spinach, and Cabbage, takes just a month to grow.

The problem is that many of these require different types of soil, excluding potatoes. This is why you need the herbology and farming books as they will help determine which foods can grow in your current environment and the environment you will be moving to.

Chapter 5 – Meat

If you have gotten all the previous bartering items and want some quick, and usually easy, to get bartering items then you have to look towards meat. Specifically, you need catch live animals rather than killing them and selling their dead bodies.

Why live animals?

Live animals are like natural refrigerators and, so long as you take care of them, they take much longer to go bad. In the event that society does not restructure itself in order to fix the problem of not having ready access to farms and other items, long term survival will depend on what you can trade. Food and access to food are the main areas of focus here. Without power, there is no way to store meat for a period longer than a couple of weeks. Sure, if you still have ziplock bags then you could store a bit of food for a long time, but these will degrade and food will eventually run out. The best way to store food for a long time is to keep the food source alive.

Capture Small to Medium

The first animals people tend to think of in this situation are either cows or deer. Cows are easy to maintain, but they're also easy to steal. Deer are neither easy to maintain or protect. Remember that in a cashless world, there are no police to prevent people from killing your livestock and taking as much food as they can. Instead, you will want to capture animals you can keep in a cage and keep close to you. These types of animals make it difficult to steal them and will usually bite hands that don't feed them as an instinctual result.

The best part is that most of the small animals can be caught, maintained, and will usually breed quickly. They normally live less than a couple of years so they breed much more frequently than larger animals. The only problem with these types of animals is that the amount of meat you get if you have barely any tools on hand is usually very small, so you will likely be trading a couple or more rather than just one. That is why breeding them matters because then you can sell more of them at a time in order to get more product.

Capturing these Creatures is Not Difficult

Most of these small to medium creatures are vegetarians with a particular taste for sweet things. All you need to do in order to capture them is to have a capturing mechanism, like a trap cage or one of the many survival traps, and some known sweet berries. This method of capturing takes very little time and can be repeated since most of the traps don't require your presence and captures them alive.

Maintaining the Livestock

Again, most of these animals are vegetarians, but it is important to realize that they also require different types of food. The most common type of staple for these are grass and leaves, but animals, like rabbits, need edible foods to grab some of the nutrients that they lack in other types of food.

Beyond that, it gets a little more complicated. If you have ready access to cages then you will likely want to build in some false bottoms on the cage. If not, then this gets a little bit harder. The smaller the animal, the more the poop, and the more unhealthy they can become both for themselves and for those who plan to eat them. Poop attracts insects, which deliver diseases they carried from other places. Likewise, it also attracts parasites and once one animal displays that they have worms in their poop then the entire batch of livestock have to be killed and cremated.

You cannot release the infected livestock back into the wild or you run the risk of infecting more animals in the wild, which is where you will be getting your next batch of livestock. Likewise, they cannot just be killed and left to rot outside for the same exact reason. The only way to be sure that the parasites don't spread is to cremate the dead animals to burn up the livestock.

You will have to remove any dead carcass immediately from the area for a few different reasons. The first reason is that it attracts bugs, which we've already talked about. The second reason is that it attracts carnivorous birds, which, like bugs, can carry diseases that are deadly to humans but not to animals. The last reason is that it attracts carnivorous animals from the direction the wind is blowing. A predatory animal knows that where there are dead bodies, there are normally live animals or animals that were there recently. The wind can carry this scent for miles before you even realize that there is a dead body. You cannot cremate them though because the smell will go even further than before.

With recently killed bodies, the smell isn't as strong and smells a lot more like burnt material. The dead bodies give off fumes, very specific odors predators know how to detect, and the fire excites the particles to make the odor more active thus spreading it even faster than before. You can burn fresh bodies, but you must take dead bodies away from the area before you bury them. While odor travels far, it also dies very quickly once the source of it is either gone or smothered. This means that burying it will smother the odor under the ground.

You will also want to inspect all of the food you give them unless you have an airtight container, but, even then, you still want to inspect it. Most of the bugs that your animals will interact with hide themselves amongst the flora that they eat. These bugs are sometimes eaten by the creatures and not only will some of the bugs make the animal sick, but they could also be carrying diseases on or in their body. Likewise, you will want to be careful of any of the food turning brown as such plants can also make the animals sick.

Lastly, you will want to wash the animals a few times a week in an area where they are not likely to be able to escape and the muck that the washing produces can be cleaned up. Animals need regular cleaning to prevent infections and diseases that could be hang out, dormant, in the dirt that's on their fur. Right now, farms tend to just hose them down but you will need to take some cloth and washing them like you would a dog. This is where they could really hurt you, so it is recommended that you wear some thick sleeves or long gloves if you have them. If you really need to, you could tie their limbs together, but this hurts the animal and the rope can open up the skin to sores that can lead to infection. It hurts the animal because they instinctively fight against being tied up.

This is all so that you keep a product that not only lasts, but builds you a good reputation of having untainted meat, something that will be a common occurrence when dealing with people who have never farmed before.

Conclusion

In this book we've covered quite a bit, but, more importantly, we have covered long lasting trading systems you can utilize to not just have something on hand to sell but something to sell continuously. This will help you live longer because it not only provides you with essential knowledge to build tools you can use but also ensures you always have something to trade if you have any materials near you.

This book is not the end all, be all of the information you will need to survive in this era of the dollar collapse but merely a powerful step in the right direction. While this book may be over, good luck and better trading.

OR Go to this URL

http://zbit.ly/1WBb1Ek

www.ingramcontent.com/pod-product-compliance
Lightning Source LLC
Chambersburg PA
CBHW051934250726
48659CB00002B/1002